What is an Ocean?

Monica Hughes

www.raintreepublishers.co.uk

Visit our website to find out more information about **Raintree** books.

To order:
☎ Phone 44 (0) 1865 888112
▤ Send a fax to 44 (0) 1865 314091
▣ Visit the Raintree Bookshop at **www.raintreepublishers.co.uk** to browse our catalogue and order online.

First published in Great Britain by Raintree, Halley Court, Jordan Hill, Oxford OX2 8EJ, part of Harcourt Education.
Raintree is a registered trademark of Harcourt Education Ltd.

© Harcourt Education Ltd 2005
First published in paperback in 2006
The moral right of the proprietor has been asserted.

Editorial: Catherine Clarke and Sarah Chappelow
Design: Michelle Lisseter
Picture Research: Maria Joannou, Erica Newbery and Kay Altwegg
Production: Amanda Meaden

Originated by Dot Gradations Ltd
Printed and bound in China by South China Printing Company

ISBN 1 844 43646 2 (hardback)
09 08 07 06 05
10 9 8 7 6 5 4 3 2 1

ISBN 1 844 43652 7 (paperback)
10 09 08 07 06
10 9 8 7 6 5 4 3 2 1

British Library Cataloguing in Publication Data
Hughes, Monica
What is an Ocean?. – (The World Around Us)
577.7
A full catalogue record for this book is available from the British Library.

Acknowledgements
The publishers would like to thank the following for permission to reproduce photographs: Alamy p. **14**; Corbis pp. **4** (Nik Wheeler), **5** (Jim Sugar), **8** (Gabe Palmer), **9** (Ralph A. Clevenger), **10**, **20** (Kevin Fleming); Getty Images pp. **6**, **11** (Photodisc), **17** (Photodisc), **18** (Digital Vision), **22** (Digital Vision) **22** (Photodisc) **23b** (Digital Vision), **23c** (Photodisc), **23g** (Photodisc); Harcourt Education Ltd (Corbis) pp. **7**, **15**, **16**, **19**, **21**, **22**, **23a**, **23d**, **23f**; NHPA (Ralph Daphne Keller) pp. **12**, **23e**; Science Photo Library (Alexis Rosenfeld) p. **13**.

Cover photograph reproduced with permission of Corbis (Craig Tuttle).

Every effort has been made to contact copyright holders of any material reproduced in this book. Any omissions will be rectified in subsequent printings if notice is given to the publishers.

The paper used to print this book comes from sustainable resources.

Contents

Some words are shown in bold, **like this**.
You can find them in the glossary on page 23.

Have you seen an ocean?

Maybe you have been to a beach and looked out across the sea.

An ocean is a very large sea.

There are oceans all over the world.

Some are warm, but an ocean can also be cold and dangerous.

What does an ocean look like?

An ocean is a huge area of water.

From under the water, an ocean can look many different colours.

The surface of the ocean is always moving.

Sometimes there are waves with white **breakers**.

What does an ocean feel like?

Some oceans feel cold, but some can feel like a warm bath.

The ocean is salty and you may feel the salt on your skin.

As the ocean moves with the **tide**, the water swirls around.

Plants in the ocean may feel slimy or prickly.

What does an ocean sound like?

When it is windy, the ocean sounds like a roaring animal.

Huge waves crash and break over rocks on the **shore**.

The ocean is much quieter when there is little or no wind.

Waves make a soft sound as they reach the beach.

How deep is an ocean?

Where the ocean meets the beach it can be quite **shallow**.

The water is a light colour and it is easy to see the bottom.

Some oceans are as deep as the tallest buildings in cities.

Where the ocean is deep, divers need lights to be able to see.

How wide is an ocean?

An ocean is so wide, you cannot see the land on the other side.

In some oceans, islands of land are surrounded by water.

There are different countries on either side of an ocean.

An ocean can only be crossed by aeroplane or boat.

What is at the edge of an ocean?

Sometimes there is a sandy beach or pebbles at the **shore**.

There are rocks and cliffs at the edge of some oceans.

There are also cities built at the edge of some oceans.

There are large **harbours** where boats can load and unload.

What lives in an ocean?

Oceans are home to lots of different plants and fish.

Coral can be found in some oceans.

Some **mammals** such as whales and dolphins also live in oceans.

Different animals and plants live at different depths.

How do people use oceans?

The oceans are used to provide food for many people.

Fish are caught in nets and brought back to land.

Oceans are also used to move things around.

Huge boats carry things from one country to another.

Quiz

Which of these plants and animals live in the ocean?

Glossary

breaker
part of a wave that crashes against something

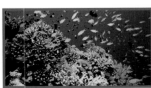

coral
tiny creatures that live in some oceans and look like colourful rocks

harbour
sheltered place at the edge of an ocean where boats and ships can come in to land

mammal
animal that feeds its young with milk

shallow
not very deep

shore
land at the edge of the ocean

tide
movement of the water in seas and oceans at different times of the day

Index

Answer to quiz on page 22

Whales, coral, fish, and seaweed all live in the ocean.